CW00495032

PRAYER & LISTENING

JAN JOHNSON

6 STUDIES
FOR INDIVIDUALS
OR GROUPS

ivp

Life
Builder
Study

INTER-VARSITY PRESS
36 Causton Street, London SW1P 4ST, England
Email: ivp@ivpbooks.com
Website: www.ivpbooks.com

While any stories in this book are true, some names and identifying information may have been changed to protect the privacy of individuals.

Originally published in the United States of America in the LifeGuide® Bible Studies series in 2020 by InterVarsity Press, Downers Grove, Illinois
This edition published in Great Britain by Inter-Varsity Press 2021

British Library Cataloguing-in-Publication Data
A catalogue record for this book is available from the British Library.

ISBN: 978-1-78974-331-9
eBook ISBN: 978-1-78974-349-4

Printed in Great Britain by Ashford Colour Press Ltd, Gosport, Hampshire

Inter-Varsity Press publishes Christian books that are true to the Bible and that communicate the gospel, develop discipleship and strengthen the church for its mission in the world.

IVP originated within the Inter-Varsity Fellowship, now the Universities and Colleges Christian Fellowship, a student movement connecting Christian Unions in universities and colleges throughout Great Britain, and a member movement of the International Fellowship of Evangelical Students. Website: www.uccf.org.uk. That historic association is maintained, and all senior IVP staff and committee members subscribe to the UCCF Basis of Faith.

CONTENTS

GETTING THE MOST OUT OF *PRAYER AND LISTENING*

For many people, prayer is a way to ask God to do what they want done. While requests are important, prayer also includes listening as we come together with God to know the "mind of Christ" about ourselves, our situations, and the people in our life (1 Corinthians 2:16). In this way prayer becomes a way of connecting with God. Through this two-way conversation God can "train [us] to be godly" (1 Timothy 4:7). God created us for a relationship with him and wants to make us into the "same kind of thing as himself."[1] Here on this earth, we become disciples of Jesus and "share in the life of Christ."[2] This transformation of your soul is "the hope to which he has called you" (Ephesians 1:18) or, more poetically, "Christ in you, the hope of glory" (Colossians 1:27).

But if we've tried to be Christlike, this can seem like a cruel joke. How do we become people who automatically love our enemies and don't grab the credit? Who naturally gives up power instead of wanting to take control? Some of us have been waiting a long time to become the tenderhearted, conscientious person our family always wished we'd become.

THE SPIRITUAL FORMATION OF YOUR SOUL

The key to this transformation—obedience—comes not from trying to be good. Trying to be good generally makes us obnoxious. When we succeed, we subtly look down on those who don't do as well. When we don't succeed, we beat ourselves up and obsess on our lack of spirituality. The enemy has won either way because we remain constantly focused on self instead of setting our hearts on things above.

So if trying doesn't work, what does? Through the work of the Holy Spirit, we copy Jesus in the behind-the-scenes, everyday activities he did to connect with God. As we let these activities become habits, we slowly are trained to have the heart of Jesus and behave as he did. As we do the connecting, God does the perfecting.

HOW SPIRITUAL DISCIPLINES WORK

We connect with God through spiritual disciplines or exercises. Prayer and listening, the topics of this Bible study, are two of them. Other disciplines include solitude, silence, Bible study, Scripture meditation, worship, celebration, prayer, service, secrecy, reflection, confession, community, and submission. It has been said that a spiritual discipline is anything that helps us practice "how to become attentive to that small voice and willing to respond when we hear it."[3]

How do spiritual disciplines (or exercises) help us connect with God?

- They build our relationship with God as we acquaint ourselves with the ways of God. (It's possible, of course, to do these disciplines in a legalistic way and never bond with Christ.)
- They build our trust in Christ. Some of the disciplines are uncomfortable. We have to go out on a limb. We try fasting and we don't die. We serve someone, and it turns out to be fun and enriching.
- They force us to make "little decisions" that multiply. Our little decision to abstain from watching a television show helps us to deny ourselves and love others in all sorts of ways.
- They reorganize our impulses so that obedience is automatic. For example, if we have a spiritual discipline of practicing the presence of God, we may learn to automatically pray the breath prayer "Into thy hands" when someone opposes us. Without our realizing it, our opponent is no longer an adversary but a person God is dealing with or perhaps even speaking through in some way.
- They help us eventually behave like Christ—but this is by God's miraculous work, not our direct effort. "The Christian thinks any good he does comes from the Christ-life inside him. [The Christian] does not think God will love us because we are good, but that God will *make us good because He loves us.*"[4]

- They teach us to trust that God will do the work in our inner being through the power of the Spirit (Ephesians 3:16). Our spirituality is not about us; it's the work of God in us. We get to cooperate in God's "family business" of transforming the world.

HOW WE GET SPIRITUAL DISCIPLINES WRONG

Spiritual exercises must be done with the goal of connecting, not for any sake of their own or any desire to check them off a list of to-do items. If we read our Bible just so we can get it done, or because we've heard this will help us have a great day, we'll be anxious to get all the Bible study questions finished or to get to the bottom of the page of today's reading. But if our goal in Bible reading is to connect with God, we may pause whenever we sense God speaking to us. Then we will study the passage further, comparing it with other sections. We'll stop and meditate on it. We may pray certain phrases back to God, indicating our needs or our wishes or our questions. We may choose to read that passage day after day for a month because God keeps using it to speak to us.

After such a session, we will have a stronger desire to connect with God. That "little choice" we made to connect will leave us slightly different for life.

The exercise or discipline is helpful because it helps us practice connecting with God. If we want to play the piano well or swing a tennis racket well, we have to practice certain exercises over and over. In life with God, we get good at connecting on an everyday basis by devoting time to developing the skills needed. Good baseball players train behind the scenes by practicing their batting day after day, with no crowds watching.[5] That's what spiritual disciplines or exercises are about. If we can hear God in prayer and in practicing the divine presence, we'll more likely hear God in a board meeting or an altercation with a recalcitrant teen when passions run high.

THE DISCIPLINE OF PRAYER

Prayer is, no doubt, the most common spiritual discipline, used even by those who aren't sure there's anyone listening! In crisis, folks who wouldn't identify themselves as Christians or who don't attend church find themselves praying. This indicates a distinct human tendency to talk to God.

While some other disciplines seem mysterious and laborious, folks almost fall into praying without thinking about it. Until we make it too complicated, that is. Over the years people have developed formulas, techniques, and foolproof schemes to get God to say yes to their prayers. It's as if God has been reduced to a vending machine, and people search for the right sort of coin to insert so that goodies will appear in the tray to be grabbed. Such frantic grasping misses the point of prayer, which is so well explained by Oswald Chambers: "We look upon prayer simply as a means of getting things for ourselves, but the biblical purpose of prayer is that we may get to know God Himself."[6]

Biblical prayer is about building a relationship with God. Knowing God himself teaches us to relate to God in an authentic way—not just doing the good things that good people are supposed to do.

We learn that God is transcendent; we learn to talk and listen to this all-knowing, all-powerful Creator in ways God teaches us. The studies in this guide outline some of those ways. We also learn that God is immanent and that we can reach out to this God who is as close as our breath.

HOW DO THESE STUDIES WORK?

These studies examine examples, how-to activities, and the results of connecting with God through prayer and practicing God's presence. One question in each of the six studies calls for actual praying to be done in the session. Look for these questions and use them. This will demonstrate the pattern that Bible study leads us to respond to God, especially through prayer.

"Now or Later" sections include activities or thoughts to experiment with in order to experience the spiritual exercise studied. At the end of the study look at these exercises and choose the one that fits you best, according to your personality or your current needs. Think of a time to try it and tell the group.

Perhaps you'll read the exercise and think it's too elementary or too difficult for you. Adapt it as needed. Or maybe you think you can guess what you'll experience, so you don't have to do it. The point is to experience it. Go ahead and try.

USING THESE STUDIES IN RETREATS

These studies work well for an individual taking a personal retreat. Simply do the studies at your own pace, and do not rush them. Allow enough time to do the transformation exercises as well. Don't feel you have to do all the studies. In fact, you may wish to focus only on one discipline and use only those studies.

A group wishing to explore certain disciplines can also use one of these studies the same way. Be sure to allow time for participants to do the transformation exercises. Some exercises may be done as a group. Others may be done individually, with group members reporting back to each other about how they heard God during the exercise.

For either type of retreat, allow plenty of time for pondering. May these studies help you move a few steps closer to living your life in union with God.

SUGGESTIONS FOR INDIVIDUAL STUDY

1. As you begin each study, pray that God will speak to you through his Word.

2. Read the introduction to the study and respond to the personal reflection question or exercise. This is designed to help you focus on God and on the theme of the study.

3. Each study deals with a particular passage—so that you can delve into the author's meaning in that context. Read and reread the passage to be studied. The questions are written using the language of the New International Version, so you may wish to use that version of the Bible. The New Revised Standard Version is also recommended.

4. This is an inductive Bible study, designed to help you discover for yourself what Scripture is saying. The study includes three types of questions. *Observation* questions ask about the basic facts: who, what, when, where, and how. *Interpretation* questions delve into the meaning of the passage. *Application* questions help you discover the implications of the text for growing in Christ. These three keys unlock the treasures of Scripture.

Write your answers to the questions in the spaces provided or in a personal journal. Writing can bring clarity and deeper understanding of yourself and of God's Word.

5. It might be good to have a Bible dictionary handy. Use it to look up any unfamiliar words, names, or places.

6. Use the prayer suggestion to guide you in thanking God for what you have learned and to pray about the applications that have come to mind.

7. You may want to go on to the suggestion under "Now or Later," or you may want to use that idea for your next study.

SUGGESTIONS FOR MEMBERS OF A GROUP STUDY

1. Come to the study prepared. Follow the suggestions for individual study mentioned above. You will find that careful preparation will greatly enrich your time spent in group discussion.

2. Be willing to participate in the discussion. The leader of your group will not be lecturing. Instead, he or she will be encouraging the members of the group to discuss what they have learned. The leader will be asking the questions that are found in this guide.

3. Stick to the topic being discussed. Your answers should be based on the verses which are the focus of the discussion and not on outside authorities such as commentaries or speakers. These studies focus on a particular passage of Scripture. Only rarely should you refer to other portions of the Bible. This allows for everyone to participate in in-depth study on equal ground.

4. Be sensitive to the other members of the group. Listen attentively when they describe what they have learned. You may be surprised by their insights! Each question assumes a variety of answers. Many questions do not have "right" answers, particularly questions that aim at meaning or application. Instead the questions push us to explore the passage more thoroughly.

When possible, link what you say to the comments of others. Also, be affirming whenever you can. This will encourage some of the more hesitant members of the group to participate.

5. Be careful not to dominate the discussion. We are sometimes so eager to express our thoughts that we leave too little opportunity for others to respond. By all means participate! But allow others to also.

6. Expect God to teach you through the passage being discussed and through the other members of the group. Pray that you will have an enjoyable and profitable time together, but also that as a result of the study you will find ways that you can take action individually and/or as a group.

7. Remember that anything said in the group is considered confidential and should not be discussed outside the group unless specific permission is given to do so.

8. If you are the group leader, you will find additional suggestions at the back of the guide.

---

[1]C. S. Lewis, *Mere Christianity* (New York: Macmillan, 1970), 162.

[2]Lewis, *Mere Christianity*, 153.

[3]Henri Nouwen, *Making All Things New* (San Francisco: HarperSanFrancisco, 1981), 66.

[4]Lewis, *Mere Christianity,* 64, italics mine.

[5]This comparison originated from and is expanded in Dallas Willard, *The Spirit of the Disciplines* (San Francisco: Harper & Row, 1988), 3.

[6]Oswald Chambers, *My Utmost for His Highest,* updated ed. (Grand Rapids, MI: Discovery House, 1992), August 28 entry.

CONVERSATION WITH GOD

Genesis 15:1-16; 17:15-22; 18:1-15

If you want a picture of what it looks like to connect with God, you might start by looking at how God interacted with someone God called a friend. One such friend was Abraham (Isaiah 41:8; see also 2 Chronicles 20:7; James 2:23).

Abraham's friendship with God was characterized by ongoing conversations. Recorded in Genesis 12–22 (perhaps many more were not recorded), these conversations are filled with the back-and-forth elements of close communication—questions, guesses, reassertions, incredulity, calculated pauses, statements of fear and doubt, careful restatements of each other's thoughts.

Yet Christians sometimes neglect to learn the art of conversation with God. Perhaps they don't feel they are "good enough" to converse with God. But if goodness were a qualification, Abraham would have been excluded. For example, just after Abraham had a conversation with God laced with miracles and visions, he betrayed a lack of confidence in God. He agreed to Sarah's scheme of conceiving a child with Hagar instead of trusting that God would miraculously provide the promised child through Sarah (Genesis 15–16). But after Abraham's attempt to "adjust" God's will, God continued to converse with Abraham. Righteousness is an outgrowth of conversation with God, not a prerequisite.

Group Discussion. What elements that make for good conversation also make for prayerful conversation with God?

Personal Reflection. What are you most likely to have conversations with God about? (Or if you don't have conversations with God, what would you like to discuss with God?)

The following three passages record a few of the many conversations between God and Abraham. In previous conversations God gave Abram (his earlier name) vast land and promised him offspring (Genesis 13:14-17). In the following conversations Abram asks God questions about these promises. *Read Genesis 15:1-16.*

1. How would you describe the interaction between God and Abram?

2. What is the first question Abram asked?

Why do you think Abram felt the freedom to ask the almighty God any question at all, even this question?

3. What do you make of God's response—not just saying words but taking Abram outside and giving him a visual metaphor (15:4-5)?

4. What does Abram's question in verse 8 indicate to you about his relationship with God?

5. If you were in a prayer conversation with God, and God said, "Know for certain that . . ." (v. 13), how might God finish the sentence? That is, what do you believe God has been trying to help you "know for certain" lately?

6. *Read Genesis 17:15-22.* What details of the covenant did Abraham question to himself and to God?

7. When has God answered you with "Yes, but . . ." (v. 19) or "I have heard you" (v. 20)?

8. *Read Genesis 18:1-15.* How did God appear to Abraham?

9. When, if ever, have you had a sense of God confronting you with a penetrating question (such as "Why did . . ." [v. 13])?

10. It's been said that humans think they are "in charge" of their prayer, relegating certain time and topics. Conversing with God means the Holy Spirit leads you, and you are no longer "in charge" of your prayer. In what ways are you tempted to be "in charge" of your prayers?

11. God's conversations with Abram were full of drama—starry nights, smoking firepots, mysterious visitors (Genesis 15:5, 17; 18:1-2). These were all props God chose for their conversations. How open are you to letting God set terms for prayer conversations with you? What prayer attitudes or activities might help you increase your openness to God?

12. The premier mark of Abraham was his complete confidence in God (faith). How might his conversations with God have developed such a faith?

Sit and reflect for a few moments. Then list a few items you would like to discuss with God, for which you would really like God's input.

NOW OR LATER

Experiment with one or more of the following.

- Take a walk and try to think of all the questions you would like to ask God.
- Pray about the self-talk that goes on in your head. Compare it with the kinds of things God often says (see question 5 above).
- Read the back-and-forth conversation in Genesis 18:20-33 and ponder why God engaged Abraham in conversation this way. Journal about whether you believe God is really interested in your ideas.

- Read Genesis 22:1-18, in which God asks Abraham to sacrifice Isaac (the son he waited twenty-five years for). In a sense God was asking Abraham, "Am I enough?" and Abraham answered affirmatively. Take a walk and consider this question from God: "Am I enough?" Answer as honestly as you can. Consider other questions: How would you be better off if God *were* enough? Are you willing to let God ask you this question for the rest of your life?

TWO

PRAYING WITH AUTHENTICITY

Psalm 74:1-23

Advice about prayer can be contradictory: "You can say anything to God because God loves you" versus "Don't be negative or despairing—remember you're talking to the God of the universe."

Authenticity in prayer is difficult. Bringing our true selves to God is tricky because God is so good and pure and we are not. Prayer is a conversation between unequals, for certain. Yet the psalms illustrate how God wants us to bring our unsanitized thoughts to prayer. We're free to state doubts, fears, and questions, yet this isn't the same as blurting out self-focused rants. We can learn to pray authentically *and* with reverence and trust.

Group Discussion. When you've heard someone pray aloud in an authentic way, how did this help you or not help you?

Personal Reflection. What settings or conditions or situations make it easier for you to pray in an authentic way to God? Why do you think that is so?

Psalm 74 is the prayer of a child of God in great pain. The powerful empire of Babylon had carried away citizens of Judah into exile after devastating the capital city and destroying God's temple. Lives of individual Israelites were destroyed, and the nation of Israel was broken.

The psalmist expresses pain and despair, asking tough questions such as "Why?" and "How long?" The psalmist accuses his enemies and states their crimes in concrete terms. But the psalmist doesn't whine ad nauseam. He focuses on God as the one in charge of the universe, reminding himself of God's great deeds and mercy in history and creation. He pleads because he knows this God is the One who can make a difference. *Read Psalm 74:1-23.*

1. What are the psalmist's doubts and fears?

In what ways can you relate?

2. If it doesn't help to ask why tragedies occur, why do you think the psalmist asks why in this psalm (v. 1)?

3. How can it be helpful to call others' sins out to God (vv. 5-8)?

4. In what ways can a person question God without being irreverent (see vv. 9-11)?

5. What references to Israel's deliverance from Egypt do you recognize?

6. How does the tone of verses 9-11 differ from the tone of verses 12-17?

7. What is the significance of the word *you* occurring ten times in verses 9-17?

8. Verses 18-23 include eight requests. What phrases in these requests fit with what we know about the character of God?

9. In what ways is this prayer (vv. 1-23) as much about God as about the dreadful circumstances of the psalmist and Israel?

10. Why is this sort of prayer likely to be healing to one's soul?

11. How is such prayer likely to result in greater trust in God and faithfulness to what God calls us to do?

12. If you were to pray at this moment, which of the elements from Psalm 74 would you like to include in your prayer?

Pick one item you listed in question 12 and write a specific prayer next to it. Then take a moment to offer that prayer.

NOW OR LATER

Experiment with one or more of the following.

- Pray, bringing a troublesome situation before God. Include as many of the elements from this psalm as you can.
- Try several postures for prayer, such as kneeling, bowing before an altar, standing with arms uplifted, standing with arms outstretched to form a cross, lying prostrate, sitting in a dark, enclosed area. Which posture helps you be authentic with God?
- Journal about what it means to be "in charge" of your prayer. How do you orchestrate, organize, and dominate your own prayers?
- Journal about how your prayer life would change if you did this: "Pray as you can, not as you can't."
- Pray the following prayer of Henri Nouwen several nights this week. Underline the phrases that best describe what you need to say to God.

> Why, O Lord is it so hard for me to keep my heart directed toward you? Why do the many little things I want to do, and the many people I know, keep crowding into my mind, even during the hours I am totally free to be with you and you alone? Why does my mind wander off in so many directions, and why does my heart desire the things that lead me astray? Are you not enough for me? Do I keep doubting your love and care, your mercy and grace? Do I keep wondering, in the center of my being, whether you will give me all I need if I just keep my eyes on you?

Please accept my distractions, my fatigue, my irritations, and my faithless wanderings. You know me more deeply and fully than I know myself. You love me with a greater love than I can love myself. You even offer me more than I can desire. Look at me, see me in all my misery and inner confusion, and let me sense your presence in the midst of my turmoil. All I can do is show myself to you. Yet, I am afraid to do so. I am afraid that you will reject me. But I know—with the knowledge of faith—you desire to give me your love. The only thing you ask of me is not to hide from you, not to run away in despair, not to act as if you were a relentless despot.

Take my tired body, my confused mind, and my restless soul into your arms and give me rest, simple quiet rest. Do I ask too much too soon? I should not worry about that. You will let me know. Come, Lord Jesus, come. Amen.[1]

[1]Henri Nouwen, *Eerdmans' Book of Famous Prayers*, ed. Veronica Zundel (Grand Rapids, MI: Eerdmans, 1983), 106.

THREE

THE PRAYER OF REQUEST

Matthew 6:9-13

For many years I've thought how lovely the prayers in Scripture are—the Lord's Prayer, prayers opening Paul's epistles. But I also thought they were so saintly that I'd never actually pray them. Prayer is supposed to be "intelligent conversation about matters of *mutual* concern," and scriptural prayers voice concerns that are deeper and richer than mine.[1] God seemed to be concerned about his will getting done, while I muddled through a normal person's everyday concerns: making ends meet until the next paycheck, getting the recognition I deserved, having a stress-free life. Where is the meeting place between the mind of Christ and the mind of me? Do we pray down and dirty or high and lofty?

But as we connect with God, God's concerns slowly become ours. In the meantime prayer becomes a meeting ground of our in-the-moment, immediate needs with God's enormously abundant life. This takes various forms. Sometimes we blurt out our raw needs and then examine them in prayer in the light of all the nurture God provides. Other times we ponder and paraphrase lofty prayers (such as the one we'll study in this session) and see that they contain nuggets of what our soul most desires—only we never saw it before. As we pray these prayers, we find that they form in us a God-drenched view of the world God *so loves*, pulling us out of our me-myself-and-I existence. By praying Scripture, in fact, we develop the mind of Christ. May that be your experience.

Group Discussion. How do you feel when you have to ask people for things? Do you feel the same way when you make a request of God? Why or why not?

Personal Reflection. What have been your most frequent prayers of request in the course of your life?

This passage, commonly called the Lord's Prayer, gives us a glimpse into the kinds of things Jesus talked about with his Father, their "matters of mutual concern." It is also called the model prayer because it guides us to consider how to pray in ways that are both lofty (hallowed be thy name) and down-to-earth (Give us this day our daily bread!). *Read Matthew 6:9-13 slowly.*

1. The Lord's Prayer is so familiar that it is often read or recited rather quickly. As it was read slowly, was there any particular phrase that stood out to you more than the other phrases?

2. How can addressing God first in a prayer (such as "Our Father") be helpful in connecting us with God?

3. How does the address "Our Father" pull us into community with others?

4. Read the following paraphrases (some expanded) of "hallowed be your name" and then offer your own:

May your name be respected, treasured, and loved.
May your name become our favorite word in our language.
Your name, your presence, and your power are so holy.

Your amplification:

5. If you were to pray that God's kingdom would come (that folks would do God's will so that love and justice, mercy and truth would be the normal state of things), what specific circumstances would come to your mind to pray about?

6. How would you complete the following personalization of "your will be done"? Reign over me! Reign over my passions, my imaginations, my senses, my ___________.

7. How would God's reigning in you this way make you more eager and more likely to connect with God?

8. Read verse 11 three times, emphasizing one of these words each time: *us, today, bread.* What different thoughts are suggested in each different reading?

9. What does God's forgiveness of us have to do with our forgiveness of others?

10. How do the requests in the Lord's Prayer work toward the transformation of our soul?

Try praying this paraphrase of the Lord's Prayer, which makes the requests in it stand out. Underline the request that is most significant for you today.

Dear Father always near us, may your name be treasured and loved, may your rule be completed in us—may your will be done here on earth in just the way it is done in heaven.

Give us today the things we need today, and forgive us our sins and impositions on you as we are forgiving all who in any way offend us.

Please don't put us through trials, but deliver us from everything bad. Because you are the one in charge, and you have all the power, and the glory too is all yours—forever—which is just the way we want it![2]

NOW OR LATER

Experiment with one or more of the following.

- Pray the Lord's Prayer, but stop after each phrase and elaborate on it. (Both Francis of Assisi and C. S. Lewis did this. Lewis called it "festooning," adding phrases that do not "obliterate the plain, public sense of the petition but are merely hung on it."[3]) For example, after saying "Our Father," stop and elaborate on "our" with "the Father of . . ." and then on "Father" with "my tender Parent whose eyes never leave me."
- Pray one of Paul's prayers for someone (Ephesians 1:17-21; 3:14-21; Philippians 1:9-11; Colossians 1:9-12) and "festoon" the phrases as you go.

- Take a walk and sing the Lord's Prayer, using one of the many melodies it has been set to.
- Write out the Lord's Prayer, inserting a very authentic personal statement after each phrase. Then look for ways this lofty phrase of the Lord's Prayer connects with your authentic words to God.

[1]Dallas Willard, *The Divine Conspiracy* (San Francisco: HarperSanFrancisco, 1998), 194.
[2]Willard, *Divine Conspiracy*, 270.
[3]C. S. Lewis, *Letters to Malcolm: Chiefly on Prayer* (New York: Harcourt Brace, 1964), 82.

FOUR

LISTENING TO GOD IN PRAYER

1 Chronicles 14:8-17

As **missionary Mary Geegh** asked God for guidance, she would sit quietly with pen and paper, writing down what she heard God say. Once when she asked for help with a colleague toward whom she felt hostility, she heard God say, "Take her a fresh egg." This seemed foolish—one egg? Why not a dozen? Would the woman laugh at her? But she obeyed, giving it to the woman's child and scurrying off. Later the woman told Mary how she'd fed all her food to her ten children that day and nothing had been left for her to eat. How she had enjoyed the fresh egg Mary brought! The hostility between the two dissolved.[1]

Many times in listening prayer God led Mary to give someone all the money in her purse (and God met her needs in other ways). One time, however, when a man came to borrow money to find his runaway daughter, Mary asked him to listen to God with her. In the silence God revealed to this man that he needed to make peace in his chaotic home first, and then his daughter would return. He did so, and she returned.

According to Douglas Steere, to listen from the heart requires

- *vulnerability*: God wants to hear my feelings, motives, and thoughts.
- *expectancy*: God will meet my needs.
- *acceptance*: I can accept whatever happens in this quiet time.
- *constancy*: I can rely on God not to get fed up with me.[2]

Group Discussion. Many people claim to have heard directly from God. What would make you believe or disbelieve such a person—circumstances? character? the person's spiritual practices?

Personal Reflection. Have you ever had a sense of God "nudging" you to do something—step out and help someone, stand up to a bully, make peace with a bully?

Having a heart of vulnerability, expectancy, acceptance, and constancy means being willing to do whatever God directs you to do. The nation of Israel faced many attacks from the Philistine army, and the previous king, Saul, was a fierce warrior who retaliated. David was a new king, and although he was a brave soldier, he responded to this attack somewhat differently. *Read 1 Chronicles 14:8-17.*

1. How do you respond to the way God answered the same question from David in two different ways?

2. What questions does a military leader normally ask when deciding whether to go to battle?

3. From what you know about David, why would he have been the sort of person who asked God questions and expected real answers?

4. What are some reasons that make "inquiring of the Lord" perhaps the last thing it would occur to us to do?

5. It's interesting that David did not rely on God's previous answer (v. 10) but inquired again. When we rely on previous answers, or answers others have experienced, what assumptions do we make?

6. Imagine for a moment that you are a soldier in this Israelite army and you actually hear God marching in the tops of the balsam trees. How might this have affected you?

What would it have been like to describe it to your children when you returned home?

7. People often expect God to answer yes or no (in this situation, attack or don't attack). How do you respond to this demonstration that God may have a miraculous detail or even a third alternative to offer?

8. Why is it sometimes difficult to follow through and do what God leads you to do?

9. What character traits would be likely to develop in a person who listened to God in prayer as David did?

10. If you were to ask God for guidance about a certain dilemma in your life, what would that dilemma be?

Read the following Jean-Pierre de Caussade quote. Then sit quietly and see if God has anything to say about what you've discussed in this study. Don't feel pressured to "hear." Just sit and wait.

> Those who have abandoned themselves to God always lead mysterious lives and receive from him exceptional and miraculous gifts by means of the most ordinary, natural and chance experiences in which there appears to be nothing unusual.[3]

NOW OR LATER

Experiment with one or more of the following.

- Sit in a quiet place with paper and pen and ask God about a certain dilemma. Write down what you hear. If God gives you direction, resolve to follow it even if it seems strange or uncomfortable.
- Reread 1 Chronicles 14:8-17. Ask God to speak to you the way he spoke to David.
- Read Psalm 81 and notice the three times the word *listen* appears. What are the benefits received by the person who listens to God?
- Review questions 4 and 6 and journal about the ideas harbored in your heart that keep you from listening to God. Which quality do you need more of: vulnerability, acceptance, expectation, constancy?

---

[1]Mary Geegh, *God Guides* (Holland, MI: Missionary Partners, 1995), 2-3, 9, 18-19.

[2]Douglas Steere, *On Listening to Another*, ed. Glenn Hinson (Garden City, NY: Doubleday, 1978), 211, 213, with my annotations.

[3]Jean-Pierre de Caussade, *The Sacrament of the Present Moment* (San Francisco: Harper & Row, 1982), 80.

PRAYING FOR OTHERS AS JESUS DID

Luke 22:31-34

Intercessory prayer (praying for others) ranges from the childhood prayer "God bless Mommy and Daddy and . . ." to the adult 911-emergency prayer "Stop my boss from acting like a pain in the neck." It's easy to miss the formational aspects of intercessory prayer—how it trains us to care deeply for others (especially when we'd like to criticize them) and prods us about how to truly love them. Intercessory prayer also forms us spiritually because it trains us to think about others through the lens of God's desire to transform them to be like himself.

Intercession is not about "patching up" folks or getting them to do what we think they should do. This is what we're doing when we ask God to help friends and family get certain kinds of jobs, to stop taking drugs, or to go back to college. Usually we've already told others to their faces what we think they ought to do, and now we offer our ideas to God. But intercessory prayer isn't about reforming people; it's about the transformation of their souls and our souls as well as we get the "mind of Christ." God may have a different plan from the one you envision. In intercessory prayer we learn to let go.

Group Discussion. How do you intercede for people without rescuing them?

Personal Reflection. Name a time when you were intensely grateful that someone was praying for you.

Jesus knew that Peter was going to deny him, and Jesus tried to warn him. He also prayed for Peter—not that he wouldn't walk through this trial but for what Peter would do in the midst of it and after it. *Read Luke 22:31-34.*

1. What seems to have been Jesus' attitude as he spoke to Peter in this passage? (See verses 28-30.)

2. Notice that Jesus called his friend "Simon" in the beginning and then "Peter" in the same conversation (vv. 31, 34). Why might he have done that?

3. Think of someone you know who is experiencing a sifting and shaking as described here: "The head and stalk of wheat were beaten and trampled and placed in a sieve. By the violent shaking of the sieve, the straw was tested for any wheat content in it. As the wind blew the chaff away, the valuable wheat emerged from the violent shaking."[1] State your fears for this person without mentioning the person's name.

4. What exactly did Jesus pray for Peter?

5. At what moments in Peter's future did it probably encourage him to remember seeing the face of Jesus saying, "I have prayed for you, Simon"?

6. Why do you think Jesus didn't pray that Peter would avoid betraying him?

7. At what points does interceding for someone cross that person's spiritual boundaries—imposing our desires to change their choices and relationship with God?

8. When does intercessory prayer become an attempt to "fix" someone—to manage or rescue that person?

9. Look at Peter's responses to Jesus' warning, as recorded in the four Gospels. What unwise attitudes did Peter display? What would have been a wiser response?

"Peter replied, 'Even if all fall away on account of you, I never will.'" (Matthew 26:33)

"Peter insisted emphatically, 'Even if I have to die with you, I will never disown you.'" (Mark 14:31)

"[Peter] replied, 'Lord, I am ready to go with you to prison and to death.'" (Luke 22:33)

"Peter asked, 'Lord, why can't I follow you now? I will lay down my life for you.'" (John 13:37)

10. How does our growth in praying the Scripture, listening prayer, and intercessory prayer help us become persons after God's heart, about whom God could easily say, "Whatever she wants, she gets" or "If he's requested it, it must be okay"? (These are paraphrases of "If you believe, you will receive whatever you ask for in prayer" [Matthew 21:22].)

Take a moment to consider someone you would like to pray for. Start by asking God to bring to mind the best way to pray for that person. Avoid "fixing" and consider how God may lead that person.

NOW OR LATER

Experiment with one or more of the following.

- Read John 17 and make a list of what Jesus prayed for his disciples. Intercede for someone you know, praying for these things.
- Sit with a photo of someone you know (or an object that represents this person) in front of you. Pray, asking God to show you how to intercede for them.
- Intercede in prayer for someone you love, praying that their faith will not fail. Tell that person what you prayed.
- Think of someone in desperate circumstances you'd like to fix or rescue. Pray instead that they will grow in oneness with God (John 17:21).

[1]Ray Summers, *Commentary on Luke* (Waco, TX: Word, 1972), 280.

PRACTICING GOD'S PRESENCE

1 Thessalonians 5:16-18

Can you identify with this description of love? "When a young man is in love with a [woman], he does not think of his beloved every instant if he has important work to do. But his devotion to her permeates all that he does with an overtone, and when a pause comes his mind naturally turns to the loved [person]."[1]

Praying continually (NIV), or what has come to be called "practicing the presence of God," involves living life on two levels, as described above in the young man's devotion to a woman. It occurs naturally, and it makes life more fun because we experience in all of life the constant companionship of the Creator of the universe, the incarnate Son, and the Holy Spirit who lives inside us. Because Jesus said, "I am with you always" (Matthew 28:20), we can say that "in him we live and move and have our being" (Acts 17:28). Enjoying God's presence, then, is one more way we can connect with God, making an awareness of God's presence a manifest reality in our life.

Group Discussion. In what ordinary situations have you had thoughts about God or wanted to speak to God?

Personal Reflection. In what ordinary situations, unrelated to church or devotional life, have thoughts of God come to you?

As the apostle Paul said goodbye to the Thessalonians, he poured forth short, pithy directions about how to live a life immersed in God. One of these instructions is to "pray without ceasing" (1 Thessalonians 5:17 KJV). If this involved a constant, uninterrupted prayer vigil, the very active apostle Paul would never have made his missionary journeys or earned a living as a tentmaker. Even avid "doers" (as Paul probably was) learn how to also "be" in life with God. *Read 1 Thessalonians 5:16-18.*

1. What three activities of the inner life are listed in these verses?

Which of these three comes most easily to you?

2. In what situation would you especially like for these three activities to be a part of your rhythm of life?

3. Look for the words in this passage that describe the all-encompassing nature of the Christian life, such as *always*.

4. Underline the words in the following passages that describe the ongoing nature of prayer.

- "We always thank God for all of you, mentioning you in our prayers." (1 Thessalonians 1:2)
- "How can we thank God enough for you in return for all the joy we have in the presence of our God because of you? Night and day we pray most earnestly that we may see you again and supply what is lacking in your faith." (1 Thessalonians 3:9-10)
- "Constantly I remember you in my prayers at all times." (Romans 1:9-10)
- "Devote yourselves to prayer, being watchful and thankful." (Colossians 4:2)
- "For this reason, since the day we heard about you, we have not stopped praying for you. We continually ask God to fill you with the knowledge of his will through all spiritual wisdom and understanding that the Spirit gives." (Colossians 1:9)
- "And pray in the Spirit on all occasions with all kinds of prayers and requests. With this in mind, be alert and always keep on praying for all the saints." (Ephesians 6:18)
- "Be joyful in hope, patient in affliction, faithful in prayer." (Romans 12:12)

These are all quotations from Paul's writing. How could these statements possibly be true?

5. Look at what is in front of you at this moment. How could you thank God for that thing or person or view?

6. What items in your home or workplace might be reminders to "hold on to a constant inner vision" of God (as Augustine said)?[2]

7. What short, three- or four-word prayers (often called breath prayers) might help you call yourself back to an awareness of God's presence throughout the day?

8. How then would you describe the process of praying continually while (pick one)

- picking out items in a grocery store?
- mowing the lawn?
- changing a baby?
- listening to the person opposite you answer the question?

9. In what sorts of situations might practicing the presence of God help you in some way?

10. How might practicing God's presence help us become more full of love or courage or purity or humility?

Take a moment to imagine yourself in a setting where you are normally busy. Pray for yourself now that as you do that task you will have a sense of God's presence and be encouraged.

NOW OR LATER

Experiment with one or more of the following.

- Take a walk for fifteen minutes, taking care to experience everything around you. Touch the plants. Gaze at the earth and notice all the shades of color. Take whiffs of the air and notice how it changes as you walk along. Use all five senses as much as you can.
- Journal about a certain situation that creates difficulty for you—talking with certain people, doing a certain task, or making certain phone calls. Now, fashion a prayer of two or three words that you could use just prior to that situation.
- Before getting out of bed in the morning, greet God with an image of him swooping down to rescue you (Psalm 18:4-19) or singing over you (Zephaniah 3:17). Before going to sleep, review your day and ask yourself, *Where did I most sense God's presence?*
- Choose three or four songs that you could hum to help you practice God's presence.

---

[1]Douglas Steere, introduction to Brother Lawrence, *The Practice of the Presence of God* (Nashville: Upper Room, 1961), 7.
[2]Augustine, *Early Will I Seek You*, ed. David Hazard (Minneapolis: Bethany House, 1991), 81.

LEADER'S NOTES

My grace is sufficient for you.

2 CORINTHIANS 12:9

Leading a Bible discussion can be an enjoyable and rewarding experience. But it can also be *scary*—especially if you've never done it before. If this is your feeling, you're in good company. When God asked Moses to lead the Israelites out of Egypt, he replied, "O Lord, please send someone else to do it" (Exodus 4:13). It was the same with Solomon, Jeremiah, and Timothy, but God helped these people in spite of their weaknesses, and he will help you as well.

You don't need to be an expert on the Bible or a trained teacher to lead a Bible discussion. The idea behind these inductive studies is that the leader guides group members to discover for themselves what the Bible has to say. This method of learning will allow group members to remember much more of what is said than a lecture would.

These studies are designed to be led easily. As a matter of fact, the flow of questions through the passage from observation to interpretation to application is so natural that you may feel that the studies lead themselves. This study guide is also flexible. You can use it with a variety of groups—student, professional, neighborhood, or church groups. Each study takes forty-five to sixty minutes in a group setting.

There are some important facts to know about group dynamics and encouraging discussion. The suggestions listed below should enable you to effectively and enjoyably fulfill your role as leader.

PREPARING FOR THE STUDY

1. Ask God to help you understand and apply the passage in your own life. Unless this happens, you will not be prepared to lead others. Pray too for the various members of the group. Ask God to open your hearts to the message of his Word and motivate you to action.

2. Read the introduction to the entire guide to get an overview of the entire book and the issues which will be explored.

3. As you begin each study, read and reread the assigned Bible passage to familiarize yourself with it.

4. This study guide is based on the New International Version of the Bible. It will help you and the group if you use this translation as the basis for your study and discussion.

5. Carefully work through each question in the study. Spend time in meditation and reflection as you consider how to respond.

6. Write your thoughts and responses in the space provided in the study guide. This will help you to express your understanding of the passage clearly.

7. It might help to have a Bible dictionary handy. Use it to look up any unfamiliar words, names, or places. (For additional help on how to study a passage, see chapter five of *How to Lead a LifeBuilder Study*, IVP, 2018.)

8. Consider how you can apply the Scripture to your life. Remember that the group will follow your lead in responding to the studies. They will not go any deeper than you do.

9. Once you have finished your own study of the passage, familiarize yourself with the leader's notes for the study you are leading. These are designed to help you in several ways. First, they tell you the purpose the study guide author had in mind when writing the study. Take time to think through how the study questions work together to accomplish that purpose. Second, the notes provide you with additional background information or suggestions on group dynamics for various questions. This information can be useful when people have difficulty understanding or answering a question. Third, the leader's notes can alert you to potential problems you may encounter during the study.

10. If you wish to remind yourself of anything mentioned in the leader's notes, make a note to yourself below that question in the study.

LEADING THE STUDY

1. Begin the study on time. Open with prayer, asking God to help the group to understand and apply the passage.

2. Be sure that everyone in your group has a study guide. Encourage the group to prepare beforehand for each discussion by reading the introduction to the guide and by working through the questions in the study.

3. At the beginning of your first time together, explain that these studies are meant to be discussions, not lectures. Encourage the members of the group to participate. However, do not put pressure on those who may be hesitant to speak during the first few sessions. You may want to suggest the following guidelines to your group.

- Stick to the topic being discussed.
- Your responses should be based on the verses which are the focus of the discussion and not on outside authorities such as commentaries or speakers.
- These studies focus on a particular passage of Scripture. Only rarely should you refer to other portions of the Bible. This allows for everyone to participate in in-depth study on equal ground.
- Anything said in the group is considered confidential and will not be discussed outside the group unless specific permission is given to do so.
- We will listen attentively to each other and provide time for each person present to talk.
- We will pray for each other.

4. Have a group member read the introduction at the beginning of the discussion.

5. Every session begins with a group discussion question. The question or activity is meant to be used before the passage is read. The question introduces the theme of the study and encourages group members to begin to open up. Encourage as many members as possible to participate, and be ready to get the discussion going with your own response.

This section is designed to reveal where our thoughts or feelings need to be transformed by Scripture. That is why it is especially important not to read the passage before the discussion question is asked. The passage will tend to color the honest reactions people would otherwise give because they are, of course, supposed to think the way the Bible does.

You may want to supplement the group discussion question with an icebreaker to help people to get comfortable. See the community section of the *Small Group Starter Kit* (IVP, 1995) for more ideas.

You also might want to use the personal reflection question with your group. Either allow a time of silence for people to respond individually or discuss it together.

6. Have a group member (or members if the passage is long) read aloud the passage to be studied. Then give people several minutes to read the passage again silently so that they can take it all in.

7. Question 1 will generally be an overview question designed to briefly survey the passage. Encourage the group to look at the whole passage, but try to avoid getting sidetracked by questions or issues that will be addressed later in the study.

8. As you ask the questions, keep in mind that they are designed to be used just as they are written. You may simply read them aloud. Or you may prefer to express them in your own words.

There may be times when it is appropriate to deviate from the study guide. For example, a question may have already been answered. If so, move on to the next question. Or someone may raise an important question not covered in the guide. Take time to discuss it, but try to keep the group from going off on tangents.

9. Avoid answering your own questions. If necessary, repeat or rephrase them until they are clearly understood. Or point out something you read in the leader's notes to clarify the context or meaning. An eager group quickly becomes passive and silent if they think the leader will do most of the talking.

10. Don't be afraid of silence. People may need time to think about the question before formulating their answers.

11. Don't be content with just one answer. Ask, "What do the rest of you think?" or "Anything else?" until several people have given answers to the question.

12. Acknowledge all contributions. Try to be affirming whenever possible. Never reject an answer. If it is clearly off-base, ask, "Which verse led you to that conclusion?" or again, "What do the rest of you think?"

13. Don't expect every answer to be addressed to you, even though this will probably happen at first. As group members become more at ease, they will begin to truly interact with each other. This is one sign of healthy discussion.

14. Don't be afraid of controversy. It can be very stimulating. If you don't resolve an issue completely, don't be frustrated. Move on and keep it in mind for later. A subsequent study may solve the problem.

15. Periodically summarize what the group has said about the passage. This helps to draw together the various ideas mentioned and gives continuity to the study. But don't preach.

16. At the end of the Bible discussion you may want to allow group members a time of quiet to work on an idea under "Now or Later." Then discuss what you experienced. Or you may want to encourage group members to work on these ideas between meetings. Give an opportunity during the session for people to talk about what they are learning.

17. Conclude your time together with conversational prayer, adapting the prayer suggestion at the end of the study to your group. Ask for God's help in following through on the commitments you've made.

18. End on time.

Many more suggestions and helps are found in *How to Lead a LifeBuilder Study.*

COMPONENTS OF SMALL GROUPS

A healthy small group should do more than study the Bible. There are four components to consider as you structure your time together.

Nurture. Small groups help us to grow in our knowledge and love of God. Bible study is the key to making this happen and is the foundation of your small group.

Community. Small groups are a great place to develop deep friendships with other Christians. Allow time for informal interaction before and after each study. Plan activities and games that will help you get to know each other. Spend time having fun together—going on a picnic or cooking dinner together.

Worship and prayer. Your study will be enhanced by spending time praising God together in prayer or song. Pray for each other's needs—and keep track of how God is answering prayer in your group. Ask God to help you to apply what you are learning in your study.

Outreach. Reaching out to others can be a practical way of applying what you are learning, and it will keep your group from becoming self-focused. Host a series of evangelistic discussions for your friends or neighbors. Clean up the yard of an elderly friend. Serve at a soup kitchen together, or spend a day working in the community.

Many more suggestions and helps in each of these areas are found in the *Small Group Starter Kit.* You will also find information on building a small group. Reading through the starter kit will be worth your time.

STUDY 1. CONVERSATION WITH GOD. GENESIS 15:1-16; 17:15-22; 18:1-15.

PURPOSE: To become familiar with prayer as conversation that involves a delightful rhythm of asking God questions and waiting on God for responses.

General Note. Conversations with God involve hearing God too. To learn more about hearing God's side of the conversation by combining prayer with Scripture reading, see the LifeBuilder *Study and Meditation* or the book *Meeting God in Scripture.*

Question 1. You may want to follow up with, What are your general impressions? This may range from surprise at how many conversations God and Abram had to how they kept talking about the covenant.

Question 2. "After this" (15:1) refers to Abram's rescue of Lot, Melchizedek's blessing of Abram, and Abram's standing up to the king of Sodom. Note that Abram's first question (v. 2) seems to verbalize the fears God was trying to allay. After God said, "Do not be afraid," verse 2 says, "*But* Abram said" (emphasis added). Apparently his fear was childlessness, and he stated it clearly with God's permission.

Question 3. Perhaps God knew the stars would be helpful because Abram, a wealthy nomadic herdsman, would no doubt see the stars every night. Each night he would be reminded of this conversation and God's promise.

Question 4. Abram must have been unafraid to express his real feelings to God. Although he "believed" God (v. 6), he also wanted assurances ("how can I know?") about taking possession of the land (v. 8). Yet Abram didn't have a God-is-my-buddy attitude either; he addressed God as "Sovereign LORD" (vv. 2, 8). Having conversation with God, then, does not mean a person demeans God's position or has license to be impertinent.

Question 5. The question is not what participants would *like* God to tell them is certain. It is not about putting our words in God's mouth. Instead, based on God's character and what God has been communicating to you, what do you think God wants you to "know for certain"? Some possible answers are

- God will never abandon you or leave you helpless.
- God wants you to change your ways about . . .
- You don't need to be afraid of . . .
- God would like to use you in a certain situation.
- God loves and forgives, no matter what.

Question 6. While Abraham's questions and laughter may have expressed doubt, H. C. Leupold comments that Abraham's laughter and talking to himself involved "joy and surprise" to match his falling on his face, an "act of worshipful adoration" (H. C. Leupold, *Exposition of Genesis* [Grand Rapids, MI: Baker, 1977], 527). He also suggests that Genesis 17:18 is not Abraham's substitute suggestion for God's idea but an additional plea. It's difficult to know.

Question 9. These questions cannot be answered quickly. Allow sufficient time for participants to think. Prepare your own answer ahead of time so that your response can jog participants' thinking. God usually catches us lying when we're pretending to be better than we are.

Question 10. If you have time, ask participants how letting God lead them in prayer makes them feel. It can be scary to consider encountering the divine in prayer and having a conversation.

Question 11. Possible responses might be:

- to ask God questions, believing that God will somehow answer them
- to quit dictating to God how to answer your prayers
- to quit filling your prayers with nonstop requests, just in case God might want to answer you
- to be open that God might speak to you through someone else—including strangers or ordinary household objects (such as a "firepot")
- to pay more attention while preparing for worship

Question 12. The back and forth of conversations involves such personal interaction that assurance and encouragement from God may be more easily sensed instead of simply being taught that God cares about us.

STUDY 2. PRAYING WITH AUTHENTICITY. PSALM 74:1-23.

PURPOSE: To understand that praying authentically involves expressing doubts and fears as well as truth, believing God can give strength and grace.

Group Discussion. Generally hearing another pray in an authentic way helps us connect with God and have a sense that the "real" me showed up and can relate to God. It could, however, be distracting for some or even embarrassing.

Personal Reflection. A special setting (church, retreat center) may make it easier to pray authentically. Being in a desperate situation often brings out authenticity.

Question 1. He fears rejection from God yet describes his people and himself tenderly as "sheep of your pasture" (v. 1). If participants mention God's anger, remind them that God's anger is not about temper tantrums or slapping folks around. It's about justice.

Question 2. He seems to be giving voice to anguish, instead of expecting a response. He's trusting an all-powerful God in asking huge, despairing questions.

Question 3. (Verses 5-8 constitute an amplification of the devastation described in 2 Kings 25:9-17, which describes the Babylonians' destruction of the temple in Jerusalem, the king's house, all the houses in Jerusalem, and the walls of Jerusalem. It details such things as the breaking into pieces the temple's bronze pillars and carrying off the special temple items made of gold.) If we call them out to God, we may be able to turn them over to God rather than call them out to others (gossip).

Question 4. This is not self-focused, exaggerated railing that goes on and on. Questioning can be done *in faith*, with the belief that God will respond. The psalmist hopes to hear from God and longs for comfort from God but is still authentic. Subsequent verses (vv. 12-17) show how the psalmist does not accuse God but ponders how God normally acts (based on God's behavior in the past) and compares it with God's seeming passivity in the present crisis.

Question 5. *Leviathan* (v. 14), according to Leupold, is another name for the crocodile, which is native to Egypt. Verse 13 refers to the crossing of the Red Sea (H. C. Leupold, *Exposition of Genesis* [Grand Rapids, MI: Baker, 1977], 538). (Remember psalms are poetry, which specializes in symbols and metaphors.) Verses 15-17 refer to God's help as the Israelites journeyed toward the Promised Land: much-needed water flowing miraculously from rocks and the Jordan River opening for them to pass (Exodus 17:6; Joshua 4:23).

Question 6. Verses 9-11 are full of despair; verses 12-17 are full of hope based on the mighty acts of God in history and creation. It appears that the psalmist is reciting the great works of God to remind himself of who God is.

Question 7. Verse 12 begins the pivot that occurs in many psalms of lament. The focus of attention shifts from being about the psalmist's dilemma to being about God. *Your* or *yours* is used three times in verses 12-17. In addition, God is addressed in verse 12: "God." Compare this with the despair of verses 9-11 and the accusations of others in verses 4-8.

Question 8. These petitions call for mercy and justice, which reflect God's character. The psalmist makes requests that honor God's covenant and causes rather than just advocating his own ideas.

Question 9. This isn't just about what the psalmist wants—a wish list for God. It considers the things God has a high regard for, especially God's covenant with Israel, which is one of the major themes of the Old Testament.

Question 10. Prayer can help us remember who God is and God's deeds.

Question 12. Encourage each member to scan the psalm and choose the element or elements they would like to include in their prayer. If they have difficulty identifying the elements, you could suggest the following:

- stating exactly what you think (including doubts and fears) with no bitterness or impatience
- pleading with God
- naming others' outrageous sins
- asking "Why?" "How long?" and other gut-level questions
- expressing confidence in God and retracing how God has miraculously helped you or others
- offering requests in the form of what you think should happen in accordance with God's character and will

When they are finished, read each of the above items and ask participants who chose it to raise their hand.

STUDY 3. THE PRAYER OF REQUEST. MATTHEW 6:9-13.

PURPOSE: To make requests of God in terms of God's concerns, not just our own.

General Note. This passage, the Lord's Prayer, is very familiar but not always understood. Help participants by reading it aloud slowly and by reading it out of a different version the second time. If you wish, also have it read as paraphrased at the end of the chapter. To prepare them for question 1, you may read it before having the passage read aloud.

Question 1. It's best to let participants tell what stood out to them without commenting. This will help them be ready to study it further.

Question 2. Addressing God is important; this is "one of the things that distinguishes prayer from worrying out loud or silently, which many, unfortunately, have confused with prayer" (Dallas Willard, *The Divine Conspiracy* [San Francisco: HarperSanFrancisco, 1998], 255). It helps us fix our minds on God, who is really present with us.

We may feel distant from God due to the phrase "in heaven." But the kingdom of heaven (or kingdom of God) is present here now (Luke 17:21). Jesus brought it in greater fullness than before, and we will experience it in yet greater fullness when Jesus comes. For now, we live in the reality of the unshakeable kingdom of God (Hebrews 12:28).

Question 3. It's tempting to think *My Father* instead of *Our Father*. "The Christian should never say *Our Father* without feeling an awakening of the love of God and his neighbor and all the reasons for it" (Jean-Nicholas Grou, *How to Pray* [Cambridge: James Clarke, 1955], 111).

Question 4. Have participants choose one of these or write their own amplification. Then pause the discussion to pray these ideas.

Question 7. As we come to believe in the magnanimous love and wisdom of God, we trust that God's will is the absolute best thing we could ever experience. We no longer see it as drudgery but as fulfillment. We long for it.

Question 8. Ask three participants to read verse 11 aloud, each one emphasizing a different word. *Us* points to community. We ask for bread for the whole world. We ask that food be distributed in such a way that those who are starving and malnourished can actually get it—either by access or with money. *Today:* I need to ask only for today because I trust that when I ask again tomorrow, God will provide. *Bread* emphasizes asking only for what is necessary for life so that we live on a "need" level, not a "greed" level. (Try adding, "I'm not asking for cheesecake or steak," and see how that feels!)

Question 9. N. T. Wright comments on the organic nature of forgiveness, which is "like the air in your lungs. There's only room for you to inhale the next lungful when you've just breathed out the previous one. If you insist on withholding it, refusing to give someone else the kiss of life they may desperately need, you won't be able to take any more in yourself, and you will suffocate very quickly" (Tom Wright, *Matthew for Everyone, Part 2* [Louisville, KY: John Knox Press, 2004], 38-40).

Question 10. We begin thinking thoughts that resemble this prayer: treasuring God's name, wanting God's will done (instead of what everyone knows I want done!), thanking God for each provision, living in the flow of God's forgiveness for ourselves and others, being grateful for all the trials and evil we're being delivered from, rejoicing that God has ultimate rule, power, and glory.

STUDY 4. LISTENING TO GOD IN PRAYER. 1 CHRONICLES 14:8-17.

PURPOSE: To bring our questions to God, being open to God's answers and obeying what we hear.

Background. Before answering question 1, you may want to offer this background: The Philistines were a constant menace to Israel. As long as David was king only of Judah, the Philistines had viewed him as an ally or even vassal. He had once been under their protection and fought with their army (1 Samuel 27–28). Once David became king over all Israel, the Philistines began to see him as a threat.

Question 1. It's not necessary to have an explanation at this point. But this does illustrate how one size doesn't fit all. God considers each situation and will help us know what to do.

Question 2. A military leader normally considers the competitive edge, comparing numbers of soldiers and weapons. Political issues usually weigh in. David was in a precarious political position, having just been anointed king over the northern tribes of Israel. Jerusalem was strategic and must not be cut off from the northern tribes. But fighting the Philistines would test the loyalty of the new citizens in northern Israel, who would have come to help. Perhaps they shouldn't be tested that soon!

Question 3. David had spent a long time in the wilderness tending sheep and developing reliance on and relationship with God. Then he'd learned to rely on God even more for practical strategies when running from Saul's relentless pursuit. It's also interesting that no messenger or prophet is named. David simply asked.

Question 4. Possible answers to the question are:

- Your mind is too full of other distractions to hear God.
- You don't expect God to speak.
- Your usual method of operation is to consult friends for guidance.
- It's easy to make up God's answer so that it agrees with what you really want to do.
- It's too easy to imagine God's answer to be the opposite of what you want because God never seems to want what you want.
- God might tell you to do something you don't want to do or don't understand.

Question 5. Possible assumptions we make might be:

- God has only one answer for every type of situation, so if something worked once, it will work again.
- If something worked for a friend, it will work for me.
- God's will is always the same in every situation, regardless of inward motives or outward circumstances.
- God isn't a personal being who examines the nuances of every situation to communicate to me a tailor-made response.

Question 6. No doubt these men were never the same after such an experience. They may have remembered this every day of their lives. They no doubt told the story to their children and grandchildren, which then increased their faith.

Question 8. Possible reasons it is difficult to follow through:

- The action God leads you to do may look silly to others.
- You are not sure it will prove helpful in the long run.
- Other people—wise people—don't agree or think the idea is odd.
- Nobody believes you got this idea from God.
- You're too embarrassed even to say you got the idea from God.

Question 10. If this is too personal, state it in vague terms: "solving a problem at work."

STUDY 5. PRAYING FOR OTHERS AS JESUS DID. LUKE 22:31-34.

PURPOSE: To make intercession by praying for others' oneness with God, not "patching up" folks or getting them to do what we think they should do.

Question 1. Shortly after, Jesus is arrested, so this seems to be a final or near-final conversation. Jesus has just noted that they have stood by him in trials and they will be honored in the future. Jesus appears to be very positive in this context just before giving Peter this prophetic warning.

Question 2. It's difficult to tell. Since Jesus seemed to use the nickname "Peter," meaning rock, to give Peter a vision of increased stability of character, perhaps he reverted to "Simon" to speak of his failure (Leo Boles,

A Commentary on the Gospel According to Luke [Nashville: Gospel Advocate, 1972], 419). Then he concluded with "Peter" to indicate that Peter would prevail.

Or Jesus may have used both names to startle Peter into remembering the time (recorded in John 1:42) when Jesus looked at Peter and changed his name. The word used for "look" is *embelpein,* which "describes a concentrated, intent gaze . . . which does not only see the superficial things that lie on the surface, but which reads a man's heart" (William Barclay, *The Gospel of John* [Philadelphia: Westminster Press, 1956], 1:74). Jesus' warning here was another heart-reading moment like the first one.

Question 4. The Greek word for "fail" means "to disappear" (I. Howard Marshall, *Commentary on Luke,* New International Greek Testament Commentary [Grand Rapids, MI: Eerdmans, 1978], 821). Jesus prayed that Peter's faith would not disappear or be destroyed by the sifting process. He also prayed that Peter would use his failure and his "turning back" to strengthen the others.

Question 5. Perhaps as he faced the amazed and perplexed crowd at Pentecost and preached (Acts 2:12-40), healed a lame man (Acts 3:4-7), was put in jail (Acts 4:2-3), or was crucified (as tradition records). If you wish, have participants shut their eyes and picture Jesus saying to them, "I have prayed for you, [your name]." Let them sit this way for a few minutes.

Question 6. Jesus had the power to stop Peter from denying him, but he didn't do this (even in prayer) because, says Dallas Willard, "it would not have advanced Peter toward being the person he needed to become. . . . How earnestly Jesus longed for Peter to come out right in his time of testing! But he left him free to succeed or fail before God and man" (Dallas Willard, *The Divine Conspiracy* [San Francisco: HarperSanFrancisco, 1998], 240).

Question 7. When we interfere in what is not our territory: another person's choices or another person's failures through which they can learn from God. Oswald Chambers warns against having so much sympathy for people as we intercede that we lose sight of "God's interest and concern for others and step into having emotional sympathy with them. [Then] the vital connection with God is gone" (Oswald Chambers, *My Utmost for His Highest,* updated ed. [Grand Rapids, MI: Discovery House,

1992], May 3 entry). God's concern is not that the people we love will have a comfortable, problem-free life but that they'll grow in oneness with him.

Question 8. We often come to God with suggestions of how God should remedy a person's plight instead of "getting the *mind of Christ* regarding the person for whom we are praying" (Chambers, *My Utmost for His Highest,* March 30 entry, italics mine).

Question 9. Peter relied on his own goodness, saying, "I'd never do that!" In less than twenty-four hours, he gave in to the taunts of a maid and betrayed Jesus. Humility and a cry for help would have been more helpful.

Question 10. Praying Scripture helps us gain the mind of Christ so we can pray for others with more wisdom because we focus on what is important—not their comfortableness or convenience but their growth in Christlikeness. (See Paul's prayers listed in the Now or Later section of study 3.) Listening prayer helps us hear what God is saying about others instead of telling God what to do about them.

STUDY 6. PRACTICING GOD'S PRESENCE. 1 THESSALONIANS 5:16-18.

PURPOSE: To practice prayer that infuses all of life as we practice the presence of God.

Group Discussion. One woman's strongest sense of God's presence came while watching the messy, gritty birth of her grandson. Others speak of sensing the marvelous rhythm of interacting with God as they garden, especially putting their fingers in the dirt, pulling out weeds, or constructing a compost heap.

Question 1. Several commentators think verses 16-18 are about the inner life while verses 19-22 refer to principles for outward corporate spiritual life.

Question 3. The words *all [circumstances]* and *continually* emphasize how these activities become part of our everyday flow of life.

Question 4. Rejoicing in the constant companionship of God and thanking God in all circumstances is a good place to begin. We can also offer requests all day long and listen all day long.

Question 7. If the group members are struggling with this, you might give the following sources.

- words of Jesus ("Into your hands")
- phrases from the Lord's Prayer ("Your will be done")
- phrases from the apostle Paul's prayers ("May love abound")

Questions 9-10. Encourage participants to be prayerful for each other as they try to answer these questions. This will give them a taste of practicing the presence of God.

Jan Johnson is the author of twenty-four books and many Bible studies and lectio divina exercises, including Study and Meditation *(LifeBuilder Bible Studies) and* Meeting God in Scripture. *She teaches at several universities as well as the Apprentice Experience. For more on Jan visit janjohnson.org.*